Divorce

Easier said than done

PRACTICAL TIPS TO HELP YOU NAVIGATE THROUGH THE PROCESS

ashley adams

Copyright © 2021 by Brandley Mill Publishing

All rights reserved.

Printed in the United States of America.

Contributing Editor: KMS

Author headshot: Peyton Adams

Cover: Megan Weaver

Paperback ISBN-13: 978-1-7344087-1-3

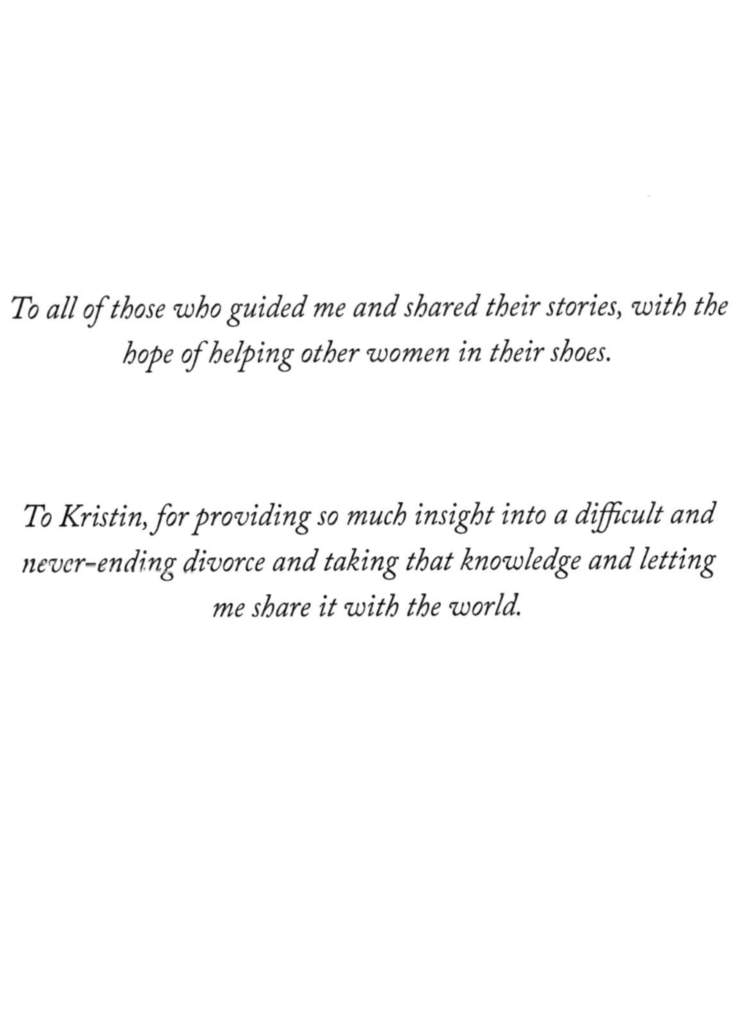

To all of those who guided me and shared their stories, with the hope of helping other women in their shoes.

To Kristin, for providing so much insight into a difficult and never-ending divorce and taking that knowledge and letting me share it with the world.

Introduction

“Accept your new normal.”

Getting divorced sucks.

Whether it was planned by you, a total surprise, or a long time coming—it doesn't matter. Your whole life is different than how it once was—how you pictured it would be.

So step one: accept that. Accept that you are embarking on an entirely different path than you were pre-divorce. For many, this is going to be one of your greatest blessings, which sounds so cruel and insane right now.

It's true though.

YOU MUST ACCEPT THAT YOU HAVE
A NEW LIFE NOW.

Until you can accept the life ahead of you, you can't fully live it. And if you can't fully live it, you can't fully find the joy within it.

I know you can do this though. I am rooting for you, and I know your circle is there for you to envelop you and support you through this. Let them!

This book is divided into three sections based on what you need to focus on right now.

11 **Legal, Tactical, and Safety:** This is the nuts and bolts of all the things that are new to you. Stuff I never would have thought of if no one told me or if I hadn't messed up on my own and lived to tell about it.

53 **Parenting:** Divorcing with children in the mix brings a whole extra level of complexity as you navigate through custody and difficult parenting. But I've got some tips here to help you not only look like the good guy to a judge but also be the better person in the process too.

91 **Recovery and Self Care:** Here's where I tell you that it gets better, and every day to come won't suck like this one does. But I'm also here to remind you of all the small things you can do to work toward this mysterious future that somehow features a happier version of you.

No matter where you are in the divorce process, this book will have something for you. Take your time, and revisit often.

Legal, Tactical,
and Safety

If you are like me, you've been thinking about divorce for a while before you actually had the conversation with your partner. If that's the case, take the time to prepare and understand your rights, the law regarding the kids, and how you will continue to pay bills and stay financially secure.

And if you were blindsided, all the more reason to start preparing now. It is never too early or too late to get organized and ready for what's to come.

If you don't already have your own bank account, please go open one and start putting money into it in a non-noticeable way. It's free to do, and I'd recommend a new bank entirely where you don't have any joint funds with your partner. Go ahead and get a PO Box at the local Post office - use this address for all the new accounts you open. Fill out a change of address form and have your mail start forwarding to that PO Box. Have a trusted friend store those documents for you. Depending on the size and where you live, a PO Box can run less than $10 a month and is worth all that and more in the security and peace of mind you will receive.

Bonus tip

When you are buying groceries or using your debit card at the store, get a small amount of cash back. Deposit the cash into your new bank account.

"Prepare."

You and your ex have a lot of history together. Stored passwords in the laptop he has? Nicknames and special dates included in your current passwords?

CHANGE THEM!

I remember the first thing I changed was our keypad to the house. I changed it to something that actually had meaning to him and I had always mocked. Something about that irony felt funny to me.

"Change all your passwords."

While you're updating those passwords, go ahead and create an entirely new email address too. If things get contentious, you're going to want to find as much privacy as you can. With many providers, you can just have emails forwarded into the same account to view. I have multiple gmail accounts, but when I'm looking on my phone, they all come into the same inbox.

Bonus tip

Think about using a private or incognito window when using your computer so the search history is not stored.

"Create a new email address that your ex doesn't have."

Work through it

New email address ______________________

New password ______________________

Did I change my email on...

- [ ] Checking account
- [ ] Savings account
- [ ] Retirement accounts (current and rollover 401k, IRA)
- [ ] Investment accounts (Bonds, E-Trade, etc)
- [ ] Insurance (Home, Auto, Life, FSA/HSA)
- [ ] Kids' Savings
- [ ] 529 Plans
- [ ] Old email address
- [ ] Credit cards (store cards, major issuers)
- [ ] Electric
- [ ] Gas
- [ ] Water

Work through it

Did I change my email on...

- [ ] Cable/Internet
- [ ] Streaming services (Netflix, Disney+)
- [ ] Car loan
- [ ] Mortgage
- [ ] Medical (Doctor, Pediatrician, Specialists)
- [ ]
- [ ]
- [ ]
- [ ]
- [ ]
- [ ]
- [ ]

Make sure that as you visit your medical professionals (Doctor, Dentist, Therapist) you remove your ex as your emergency contact. Be sure that your ex can no longer access your personal information.

Additionally, make a note to yourself to remove your ex as your beneficiary. In most states, you cannot do this until you are legally divorced.

“Remove your ex from your emergency contacts.”

Things vary so much depending on your state and the cause for divorce. For example, my divorce was handled completely through family court because it started with a protective order. But most divorces are handled in civil court, by the same judge who may have been sentencing traffic offenses the hour prior.

“Understand the legal process.”

This is your divorce. As much as you may want to hide under the covers until it's all over, you can't afford to do that. You get one good shot at a custody agreement and separating the assets. Yes, things can always go back to be revised in the future, but it's nearly impossible unless something truly horrible happens with the parent. Now is your chance.

Don't be passive and rely on your lawyer or mediator completely. They can guide you, but you need to be the one to make the decisions and fight for what matters most to you. Ask a lot of clarifying questions so that you completely understand what your options are and what your choices mean.

“Be an active participant in your life.”

This is so much easier said than done, but it is SO IMPORTANT!

Don't let him get you to engage in back and forth via text or email. Let him be the one to look like an ass. It's so easy to get feisty in a text or an email and shoot it off without a thought, but how would it look in front of a judge? In front of your teenager?

Always do your best to stay composed when engaging in anything written. Be the responsible and loving parent.

Bonus tip

Never respond to an email or text right away! Most messages do not need an immediate response. Set a cool off period. Maybe it's an 8 hour time limit or 48 hours. Whatever it is, stick to it! You are so much wiser after you cool off. I have a friend that actually took off email from her phone. This way she didn't get a notification that may ruin her day. She set a time—eg. Tuesdays at 8pm, when she would check that email address then she would respond on Thursdays after she cooled off.

Keep your cool.

When you're in the divorce process, or just beginning to think about separation, there can be a lot that needs to happen, and if you try and tackle that all at once, it could feel overwhelming. Make your list and start crossing things off. Just take it one day at a time.

Or don't make a list. That may really make you overwhelmed. But just know that a lot of the legal stuff can feel like you have to rush—but you are in control. Some things like discovery by the opposing counsel has to be submitted quickly or you face contempt of court. Just know what has mandatory deadlines and create a manageable to do list to start tackling it.

This is your life. Don't forget, we already talked about not being a passive player in this process. If you're overwhelmed, choose one small task to take care of today. Just one. Don't throw your hands up and just say you can't do it.

“Take action everyday to move things forward.”

what do you need to do

Work through it

Need to do	Deadline	Optional/Required	Completed
Complete discovery	Jan 8th	Required	✓
Call dance about scholarships	Jan 21st	Optional	

We've already talked about changing passwords. Now we're talking locks. Keep your home safe. Avoid any possibility that he could come in without an invitation. Even if things are civil, if you have stayed in the home and that's agreed upon, then you have the right to change the locks.

It's not just about feeling safe or being smart, there's a great sense of peace and independence about it too!

Bonus tip

If you have a restraining order, tape a copy of it to the door or window. If he ever tries to call a locksmith to get in, the locksmith will see the order. Otherwise, your ex can present his driver's license with your home address on it and get access to the house.

“Change your locks.”

Study up. If your battle drags on for years, it could wipe you out financially. I've seen it happen with more than one person. I have a dear friend who eventually stopped paying a lawyer because she'd learned so much on her own, and quite frankly, couldn't keep up with the constant bills thanks to her ex who was being bankrolled by his parents.

Court documents require a lot of technical knowledge, but it's certainly stuff you'll pick up over time if you find your case dragging on.

Another idea is to do a lot of the leg work for your lawyer—like drafting documents. Then have them review for a fraction of the price and you can submit them yourself.

Bonus tip

Some lawyers bill you by the hour and others bill by the job. You will want to weigh the pros and cons of each billing method to decide what works best for you. Every time you text your attorney when you pay by the hour could be a billable charge—one text at $295 an hour equals a bill for $29.95. If you are one that feels better with constant communication with your attorney, you may want to opt for an attorney that can charge by the service provided.

Lawyer up.

If mediation is an option for you, try it! There's nothing to lose, and if you can agree on an outcome, then you can save yourself a lot of money—which means more for you to begin this next phase of life with and more for your future and for your kids.

Mediation is free in most states, and you can still consult a lawyer even if you are going this route.

You will want to make sure that your agreement is written with specifics. If you agree to dad getting kids one night a week during the week and every other weekend - define the times. You can always agree to a change later but have defined terms in writing so there is a solid foundation of rules that you both must follow.

If the agreement just says "every other weekend"—when is that? Does that mean starting Friday after school or does the weekend start on Saturday morning? Also, try to get authority to have the final decision in case you don't agree. Meaning, if the order says "mom and dad have joint legal custody with medical decisions" and a kid needs braces, you both disagree on which orthodontist to use - who has final say? Or do you continue arguing while your kid's teeth remain untreated?

“Request mediation.”

Stop. Collaborate. And listen.

Stop	*Is this text helpful and necessary?*
Collaborate	*How can you work with your partner in this moment?*
Listen	*Say it out loud. Do you sound selfish, evil, or petty?*

Texts and emails end up in domestic court cases ALL THE TIME.

Focus on the facts and check your emotion at the door.

If this is a struggle for you, have a trusted partner read each text before you send it. A second set of eyes to read it in a different tone is very helpful.

> “Always write out your texts and emails as if the judge will read them aloud in court. Be as objective as possible.”

What does limited and essential contact mean? Basically, only talk when it's necessary for the kids, moving the divorce along, or helping you separate your assets.

While things are heated and hard, this works wonders. It also helps you keep a clear head and not let yourself get sucked in to a certain look or emotion he can pull out of you that makes you feel confused, in love, or more angry.

For the first 6 months of my separation, I had a protective order in place, which meant my ex and I were not allowed to talk or be around each other. There were many times I knew it was no longer necessary, but it was incredible leverage for my mental health. I felt so much pity for my ex and the addiction he was facing, and even though I knew I wouldn't have taken him back, I didn't want to take on the extra pain and empathy by being around him and talking to him.

"Stick to limited and essential contact only."

After a divorce, you have two rents or mortgages, two utility bills, two cell phone bills. Things that used to be cheaper as a couple are now doubled in a divorce.

Be mindful of your financial situation and identify where you may need to make cuts. Maybe you didn't have to budget much before and now those mindless trips to Target require a little more thought. *(Sorry to break that one to you. I promise, you can still go to Target. Maybe just make a list on occasion.)*

"Think about the cost of your new life."

The job of a good mediator or collaborative lawyer is to help two people work together for a positive outcome without going to court. Court is only going to lead to more distrust and frustration since a court attorney is typically not as well-trained in de-escalating conflict like a mediator.

To help move the mediation along with some agreements, list out some things that you think your soon to be ex will want that you don't care about. Then you can offer these as negotiables for things that you really want. Also rank your most important must haves. You've gotta prepare yourself though. You will most likely not get everything that you want.

“You can still mediate even if you don’t speak to the other person.”

Here are some examples of things to think about in negotiations…

Work through it

What are my MUST keeps from the house?

Do I really want the house? Or would I rather have cash to purchase/rent a new home?

Do I really want the car?

Where is my Grandmother's china? Meaningful items?

What about the Christmas decorations? Should we split them?

Once the paperwork is signed—divorce is final, custody order is official—STOP fighting!

Every time your ex pushes your buttons and you want to retaliate with words—STOP! The fight is over! The judge has made the decision. Just stop fighting.

Don't engage in that behavior. It only makes you upset, and it hurts the kids. When you engage, you give your ex exactly what they want. They want to upset you, and you proved to them that they did. Don't give them that!

Remember that journal I mentioned? This is a great time to get it out—vent away!

“Once the paperwork is signed, stop fighting.”

Who managed the bills while you were married?

Who checked your banking app daily looking at various accounts?

If you did, then snaps to you. You're 100 steps ahead. If you didn't, learn how.

This stuff is all about organization. If it's easier, start paying with cash. Figure out what you've been spending on food, gas, eating out, Target (obviously its own category), and so on.

Then figure out what may be more realistic. Can you buy store brand instead of name brand? Can you do more grocery shopping from a place like Aldi or Lidl?

There are a ton of great accounts you can follow on social media with fantastic tips on how to budget, even as specific as budgeting as a single parent!

“Get organized financially.”

Parenting

If you're in a position to safely do so, give your kids the courtesy of sitting down as a family to share the news that you are getting divorced.

Not only does this help them hear a more balanced message since you're both present, but it allows you and your soon-to-be ex this one moment to see how this is going to impact the kids.

Hopefully, it's a moment that the two of you can hold on to as you both think about the entire divorce proceedings and what you're fighting over and who you are fighting for.

“Tell your kids the news together if you can.”

If you're going through a divorce, do everything you can to keep some normalcy in your life. The kids are already facing a huge change in their home, so think about what can stay the same and hone in on that.

This is where being a single mom gets tough. Your kids usually just want their "normal" life back, and they can't have it. Even if you are struggling financially, what can you keep "business as usual" for them?

Does the dance studio offer scholarships? Can your church help you with soccer fees? Is there a moms group with funds to give? There are so many resources within local communities, but the hard part is when we don't know where to look. Or we are embarrassed to ask.

If you don't know where to begin, your local moms Facebook page is probably a good starting point. Most of them allow you to post anonymously if you are not ready to admit to the entire world you need help.

“Look for normalcy in your life.”

This was one of the greatest tips I got when I went through my divorce.

I had a small daily planner where I wrote out everything:

- Times he failed to show
- Times I thought he was intoxicated
- When he lashed out at me
- Comments from his family or friends that supported my case

The list goes on. Use it to log any issues that come up with your ex. Having a record of every time he bails on the kids or fails to do something he says will help you so much when it comes to court proceedings.

Take time everyday to update your planner—you have so many moving parts that things will quickly get away from you if you don't do this daily.

“Get a planner.”

This is the easiest thing to say and one of the hardest to do—especially when you have a kid who idolizes their dad and has no idea what he's really like.

I'm talking about the loser who hits you, is out getting drunk, can't hold a job—and you've been such a good mom that you have completely shielded your kids from that.

One day, they'll know the truth. Now just isn't that time. Let them maintain their innocence as long as they can, mama. You can do this!

If this one is especially hard for you, you may want to start a journal to your kids.

Grab a blank journal and write to them what you would love to say and why you are not saying it to them now. This will allow you to get it out of your head and heart without passing the hurt onto your kids.

This journal may or may not be something that you ever share with your kids. Obviously, you do not share this with them while they are still children.

“Take the high road.”

Spending time with your kids may sound too simple.

You say, "My kids are with me all the time!"

But are you really spending time with them?

Be engaged with them.

You are busy! You are handling everything on your own—but you must have quality time with the kids that you are working so hard for.

Make routines—bedtime story, breakfast at the table with no devices, daily devotions, something that they can count on to know that they'll have with you.

If it's new for you to start doing this, give it time for the kids to start recognizing it as a habit and not a one-off. You will LOVE the shift in behaviors!

“Spend real, quality time with your kids.”

Work through it

What are the quality time habits I am going to start?

Dinner at the table without devices and ask about the best part of their day.
Color a picture and then share what you drew.
Talk about the sermon we heard at church this week.

Mama, it is THE WORST to leave your kiddo. The worst. But then worse than leaving them is that weird feeling you get when you get just a few hours to breathe and have a break.

As moms, it feels like we should be there for our kids in every moment of every day, and it's DRAINING. As much as we love them, doing it on our own is so damn hard. And you mamas who do it without family nearby—BLESS YOU!

So when your kids can't be with you, please promise me you'll have a good cry but then pick yourself right back up and go get a pedicure. Or take a nap. Or go out for drinks with a friend. Just do something all about you.

I'm partial to Netflix marathons, ice cream, and queso dip. Sometimes I hang out with a friend, but honestly, I just like to have the quiet. You do you.

> “Practice self care when you don’t have your kids with you.”

Work through it

When I don't have the kids, I promise to...

Get a Pedicure

Read "The Other Side of the Door"

Watch 3 episodes of The Bachelorette

I promise you, your ex probably isn't thinking how great you are if you play nice. He's thinking that he can walk all over you and you aren't strong enough to stand up to him.

STAND UP.

Do what you need to fight for your kids and yourself.

There's a difference between doing what's best for co-parenting and being extra nice in co-parenting thinking it will help down the road.

That "being nice" can be a slippery slope to getting walked on. Do what needs to be done to give your kids the best co-parenting situation you can.

> “Don't believe that if you play nice that it will be better for future co-parenting.”

It's SO easy to get worked up over your ex. That's part of why they are your ex. And when you go all Mama Bear on them, it's never a good look.

The best thing you can do is keep communication to the must haves, and even better, use an app like TalkingParents, which can store all calendars, messages, and phone calls—and its contents are generally admissible in court.

Or OurFamilyWizard, a similar app, that uses machine learning to track the emotional tone of your message and tells you if it comes off as rude or aggressive! Technology is awesome sometimes! It also time stamps when the other person saw an email from you, so they can't falsely claim they never saw or received it!

P.S. Apps come and go all the time, so if these no longer exist when you need them, a quick Google search will point you in the direction of something similar.

“Communicate with your ex as if it's a business relationship.”

I kept many of our family traditions for stability (and because they were traditions I loved too!), but I also started new things for the holiday season too.

This is a time when Pinterest really can help you become creative without a lot of skill or money.

A few fun ones:

- *Make reindeer food (oats, glitter, sprinkles, etc)*
- *Have your elf bring the kids Christmas pjs to wear during the season*
- *Decorate cookies*
- *Make a handprint canvas print (Hearts with their feet, a turkey with their hands)*

Sometimes new memories forged through difficult times can become the most treasured ones, and I have no doubt you're going to make it an incredible year, mama!

“If this is your first holiday apart, start a new tradition with your kids.”

Sometimes it's okay to tell your kids what's going on. You can sit them down with the facts. Only the facts—no emotion, no opinions, just the black and white facts.

"Here is the custody order, also known as the rules that your [other parent] and I must follow. It says that you are with me at this time on this day—you haven't been because your [other parent] is not following the rules. In this case, the rules are law. They are breaking the rules that a judge told them they had to follow—they can be punished for not following the rules."

Obviously the age of the child plays a role in how much to say. And this does not ever have to be a conversation you have, but if your ex is causing chaos by not following the custody order or child support order... tell the child the truth. It is their life too—they have the right to understand what should be occurring.

> "Sometimes it's okay to tell your kids what's going on—as long as you keep it based in fact."

Eat healthy! It's so easy to live by snacking especially when you are juggling so much—but make sure YOU sit down with the kids and eat a meal when you are feeding them!

This is time you can have with your kids and stay healthy too. Not to mention—it's much easier to force your kids to eat their veggies when they see you eating yours!

“Eat a family meal together.”

Work through it

This may be the time to start meal planning—don't just throw the frozen chicken nuggets into the microwave every other night. Plan out your meals. They can still include things like dinosaur chicken nuggets, but just make sure you are all actually sitting and eating your meal together (and planning what goes with it).

List your meal ideas here, then plan out a sample week and grocery list on the next page

One Week Plan

SUNDAY

MONDAY

TUESDAY

WEDNESDAY

THURSDAY

FRIDAY

SATURDAY

Grocery list

Don't forget to take your schedule into account while you plan. What nights will you be eating on-the-go due to soccer practice or piano lessons? When will it be just you at home?

Gosh, this feels counter intuitive. I wanted so badly to give the kids time with their dad (who was mostly absent), so when he asked to go have lunch with them or come over after work, I would happily say yes.

But for many of you, you're fighting a hard custody battle (my ex had no overnights and only supervised visitation), and during the battle (and it ***is*** a battle!), it's easy to be "nice" and then have it perceived a different way in court or by your ex.

Once you start being flexible, they try and gain more and more from you.

Stick to the court order for now.

Get in your groove.

Once that is established and set, you can eventually loosen up a bit and work together better, hopefully!

"Flexibility is your enemy."

I admit, I still cringe and get real judgmental when I see people jumping in to new relationships post-divorce. Obviously, I may not know all of the steps they went through to heal, and I always pray that they have. I hope for the best. But I mostly pray that the kids will be okay.

It is never easy on a kid to have a new adult figure enter their life. My kids were 2 and 5 when they met my now-husband, and that was hard for the totally opposite reason it probably would be for teens—my five year old was begging me to marry him after a month of knowing him. It was mortifying. And then, a year later when we were engaged, she suddenly realized he'd be disciplining her and she was not on board with that.

It's been a long road filled with lots of big emotions. You'll likely face those erratic emotions from yours too. Just have patience and grace with them.

For me, it always came down to this:
How much am I willing to break their hearts all over again?

And be careful—

Don't ask your kids if they are okay with you dating this new person unless you are ready to end the relationship when they say no. It is great to talk to your children about their feelings about this new person in your life, but in many cases, your child may feel like you are picking the new guy over them and their expression of emotion may be a bit displaced.

“Really think about when to introduce a new partner.

The key to setting those limits is to remember it goes both ways. You have the right to include in the agreement that non-related adult sleepovers cannot occur at the same time as the children being there.

This can sound great in theory, especially if you are worried about a cheating partner moving on quickly and exposing the children to that. But what if you decide to never remarry and have a long-term partner instead? What if you are engaged?

This one is a slippery slope and the enforcement goes both ways. It's also *tough* to enforce. However, it may work in your favor as a negotiating point, so definitely consult your lawyer on how to proceed with the language of this if it's something you feel passionate about.

> You can place limits in your divorce decree on how you and your ex are allowed to involve future partners.

Let's say your kids are 5 and 7 now.

They may have soccer once a week and an occasional playdate. But what happens when they are 12 and 14? Maybe a weekend that belongs to you is when they really want to have a sleepover with a friend, or they have an out-of-town swim meet.

What if the only time a tutor has available is Wednesday night when dad is supposed to take them out to dinner?

These are real life situations you're going to face.

You need to both make sure you're allowing for their growth, their happiness, and their health—even if it means less of "your time."

“Stick to your schedule, but be flexible as your child grows.”

Recovery and
Self Care

Trust your gut!

For months, I knew my ex-husband had more than just run-of-the-mill anxiety. I knew it was from drinking, but I just couldn't prove it.

When it turned out that my gut was right, I was furious with him and with myself for putting our kids in so many dangerous situations.

If you feel like something is wrong, it probably is. Now, you have to decide how to manage that stress and what modifications you want to make to your life in case you are right.

“If you aren't sure where to begin, start by trusting your gut.”

I am now a two-time published author all because I journaled while going through my divorce.

My brain was firing out so much and I couldn't keep up with the emotions and words. So for me, sitting down after I put the kids to bed and typing it all out into a word doc worked best for me. I really wanted to be someone who wrote it out in a beautiful journal. I'd been gifted so many! But it wasn't enough for me to get it all out.

In the early days, you'll probably have plenty of thoughts to get out. Take time every day to write. One of the most powerful parts of journaling is going back to see what you felt in a given moment and looking at your growth. Soon, those daily entries will become every few days, then once a week.

These days, I don't write much at all. I'm able to get out my thoughts through a gratitude and prayer journal instead.

Write.

The weird thing about grief is that you never realize you've switched to a new phase of it until you're knee deep into it. I used to cry on my way to work every single day (thank you, Sara Evans for the best break up anthem of all time) until one day I realized I hadn't cried in weeks.

WHEN DID THAT HAPPEN?!

I knew I was on the verge of losing it just yesterday, right? But it really wasn't ***just yesterday.*** I can transport myself back into that place of hurt and pain in a heartbeat, but the reality is that I don't feel that way anymore.

That small amount of healing that takes place every day eventually becomes giant leaps when you look back to where you were 3 or 6 months prior.

That's not to say that you won't have all new forms of grief forming all the time during the first year or two, but they'll change—and what brings you to daily tears today won't be causing those tears 6 months from now.

Just keep swimming. Just keep swimming. Just keep swimming.

You've got this.

“Things will get better. You won’t always feel the way you do right now.”

I was only 31 when I separated from my husband. I didn't know anyone my age who was divorced, so when I learned about DivorceCare at church, I thought it would be filled with people I couldn't relate to. They'd all be too old. They didn't try hard enough. Someone cheated. There was no love.

The excuses to not participate are endless, but at the end of the day, the core reason you are all brought together is what will bond you, and the differences are what will help you grow and learn the most.

Every group is different, and I even led DivorceCare twice after I went through it as a participant. What I noticed is that age wasn't the biggest factor in bonding— it was the shared experience. Fighting for custody, domestic abuse, addiction, infidelity... they were all unique reasons that led to divorce, yet we all also faced similar issues and feelings.

Just being able to sit in a room and hear that others can relate to you (when it feels like NO ONE can!), it was life giving.

And it didn't hurt that I came away with a couple of incredible friends.

Find a support group.

Even if you don't feel like talking, listening can help just as much.

Who is that person who you can confide all your ugly truth to? The one that will be honest with you—cry with you and also tell you when to get off your ass. This person may be someone you haven't met yet, or it could be an old friend. Maybe even a family member. Whoever it is, find them and let them know—you're my person.

This is more than a support group. It's your PEOPLE. Who can you let be honest with you? Cry with you but still give you the tough love when you need it?

“Identify your people.”

Work through it

Who are my people? What can they help me with most?

Name	Why
Ashley	She has been divorced
Emma	Her dad was an alcoholic

Social media is the perfect place to go for funny videos and pictures of cute kids. Then it gets quickly ruined with political posts or people "vaguebooking" about random things happening in their life to their 700 "friends."

Please don't be one of those people.

Don't say things like, "*I can't stand when people say they will do something for your kid and then never show up.*"
(bashing ex = no no)

And don't say things like, "*Oh, it's so hard to see all the happy couple posts for Valentine's Day. Must be nice.*"

Come on, now!

How do you react in your brain when you see stuff like that? You don't want to be that. Use your people and your support community.

If you really have the urge to vent on social media, I'm a big fan of closed Facebook groups. I'm in a great single mom one that has the occasional outburst post looking for validation and solidarity, but most of the posts help center me and bring me back to my reality. It's just enough to make me realize that (a) I'm not alone, and (b) it could be so much worse.

“Keep it off social media.”

Some days, what you're going through will seem impossible.

On those days, just take baby steps (from your bed to the coffee maker may be enough).

Other days, you can take more. You can control you during a time that seems like your life is out of control.

Say it with me:

I CAN CONTROL ME!
I CAN DECIDE TO MOVE FORWARD!
I CAN MOVE MYSELF!
I CAN!

Repeat. Repeat. Repeat.

Say it out loud.

Write it on your mirror.

Write it on your hand.

Sticky note on your car dashboard.

Wherever you need the reminder.

I CAN DO THIS.

“Take control of you!”

There's something SOOOO wonderful about a good cry fest. Sometimes I find it therapeutic to put my mindset in an emotional place so I can tap into something I've been avoiding or too busy to let my mind react to.

Crying doesn't have to be a sign of weakness. Sometimes, it's when you find your strength.

Cry.
Let it out.

Work through it

What do I need to let myself cry about?

I know, you just want to sit with that gallon of ice cream and a spoon and watch reruns of The Office, but for real—your body works SO HARD when you're going through a traumatic event that it's even more important than normal to find ways to get in your fruits and veggies and to minimize the junk.

May the force be with you on that one because Lord knows that ain't easy!

Eat healthy.

Is it a new found love of the gym or running?

Screaming ugly words into a private journal?

Punching your pillow?

Maybe you're going to start knitting or needlepoint?

Find a **HEALTHY** outlet.

You need one in the best of relationships, and you really need one now.

“Find your outlet.”

Work through it

What can I do?	When can I do it?
run	9am when kids get on the bus
write	8pm when kids go to bed
sing angry songs in shower	EVERY SHOWER!

Turn your head up and talk to God.

Even if you aren't religious today, this is a great time to consider it. He is a great listener and an awesome provider.

For so many of us, we didn't even find our way into a church until our divorce. I promise, this is the best time to start hanging out with the big man upstairs. It changed my life and made my healing process so much better than it might have been otherwise.

There's a reason pastors talk about church being for broken people. It's how most adults ended up going in the first place!

Pray.

Exercise.

I know, I know.

Again, it's the couch and ice cream and Netflix thing.

But really, even if this means daily stretching or foam rolling or lying in child's pose for 27 minutes—you've got to invest in your body and keep it strong.

The same way it needs good nutrition, it needs good love for its muscles and heart.

“Move your body daily.”

Feeling thankful in the midst of change and pain can be hard, but it's crucial to keep your mindset positive with a grateful heart.

As you begin thinking about the big events you now have to split, it can be hard to find gratitude. Many separated and divorced kids spend holidays with only part of their family.

Maybe this is your year.

Maybe not.

Maybe it's your first year trying to navigate that.

One of the biggest practices I've held onto is a journal I (try to) write in every morning. I just list 5 things I'm grateful for from the last 24 hours. I'm talking things like, "I got to sit by the fire and read a book for an hour" or "I hit green lights the whole way home."

Take 5 minutes today to think about what you're grateful for in this moment. Hold on to all the positivity you can.

“Practice gratitude.”

Okay, it doesn't have to be The Bachelor. If that's not your jam, don't get caught up in the reference.

What I mean is, now that you're separated or getting divorced, what's something that you loved and gave up because he didn't?

Maybe that was hiking or biking.

Maybe it was eating Indian food or full fat cream cheese.

Maybe it was getting sucked into trash tv and loving every second of it.

My point is, YOU can decide if you want to spend your Monday nights with The Bachelor or your fridge full of fat free salad dressings.

Just you. No ex to consider.

Either way, think about your passions and interests and find a way to bring them back into your life.

You deserve them.

“

He thought The Bachelor was stupid... now you can binge watch 27 seasons.

Really take the time to figure this out so you don't repeat mistakes in your next relationship.

That right there is probably why second marriages are even more likely to end in divorce than the first.

I heard a stat that over 80% of people walked down the aisle knowing they were probably making a mistake.

Now, maybe that's all said in hindsight, but it was true for me. I had cold feet for months leading up to my wedding because I watched my fiancé spiral in depression after he lost a family member and was drinking heavily, but then I pushed through thinking it was just grief, not the signs of addiction.

In my case, I had a fear of being alone and never getting my fairy tale ending with kids and a real, grown up life.

As I worked through all of this in my divorce, I learned more about what I wanted in a partner and felt completely okay knowing I probably wasn't going to get remarried.

The feeling of being content in my life was a key to my recovery and movement through the healing process.

And figuring out that key *for you* is going to be essential to your recovery.

“

Understand why the marriage is ending.

Work through it

Some things to think about as you're trying to recover:

- Don't make any life decisions for at least a year.
- Consider finding a therapist, divorce coach, or support group. Even on Instagram! Do a quick search.
- Pay attention to any new pains, aches, etc and write down what was happening around that time.
- Journal. Some people say you should write for 30 minutes a day because it's when you run out of things to write that the real juicy stuff makes its way to the surface.

Y'all.

If you are as nosy as I am, then it feels like it takes years off your life to restrain yourself from pumping your kids or friends for information on your ex.

Don't. Do. It.

A little bit of info only makes you want more.

And how often do your kids get 90% of the details of a story wrong?

Add that to the plus column for not sharing details on a new boyfriend with your kids, so they don't share details back until you're ready.

Don't ask.
Don't tell.

I don't know where you are in the calendar year as you're reading this, but the turn of a year is always a beautiful time to reflect on your year and your life.

Whatever the year brought you—personally, professionally, or medically—it's time to focus on the future.

The possibility.

The hope.

You control what YOU control. Not your ex. Not your mom. Not your boss. You.

If you don't know how to do that, I suggest some visualization.

We've talked about gratitude practices already, but you can take that a step further and think about how you envision your future.

Each day, I write down the same set of goals I hope to make come true in the next ten years—and I write them as if they have already happened. It's a great way to help manifest dreams into reality.

You got this.

Let's kiss the year goodbye and welcome in a new season with some bubbly and a slice of optimism.

“Head into the new year with a new mindset.”

Work through it

What are my dreams for the future?

What do I want to accomplish this year?

What about in 5 years?

Personally, I write my dreams and goals as if they have already happened. Something like, *I work out every day*, or *I work for myself.*

You may be the only person you know who has gone through a divorce, or you may know several.

Part of what made me so willing to share my story is how alone I felt going through the process.

I was only 31 and didn't know anyone yet who had been through it. If I hadn't been dragged to DivorceCare and found women to connect to, I don't know where my healing journey would have led.

But now, I am so honored to help others and offer to sit with them in the hurt and loneliness, holding space for them.

Every experience is different, but the emotional support and advice you can offer someone is going to be invaluable to them.

You've grown and you're better than ever. It's time to share that and give someone else hope who isn't as far along in their journey.

Thank you in advance for helping in the next person's recovery.

“Pay it forward.”

I will survive this.

I am strong enough for this.

I will get better.

I will laugh again.

I will be happy again.

I am loved.

www.ingramcontent.com/pod-product-compliance
Lightning Source LLC
LaVergne TN
LVHW010623100826
845148LV00014B/3084

* 9 7 8 1 7 3 4 4 0 8 7 1 3 *